EARTH IN ACTION

EARTHQUAKES

by Carla Mooney

Content Consultant
Stephen A. Nelson
Associate Professor of Geology
Tulane University

CORE
LIBRARY

Published by ABDO Publishing Company, PO Box 398166, Minneapolis, MN 55439. Copyright © 2014 by Abdo Consulting Group, Inc. International copyrights reserved in all countries. No part of this book may be reproduced in any form without written permission from the publisher. The Core Library™ is a trademark and logo of ABDO Publishing Company.

Printed in the United States of America,
North Mankato, Minnesota
042013
112013

Editor: Lauren Coss
Series Designer: Becky Daum

Library of Congress Control Number: 2013902045

Cataloging-in-Publication Data
Mooney, Carla.
 Earthquakes / Carla Mooney.
   p. cm. -- (Earth in action)
ISBN 978-1-61783-937-5 (lib. bdg.)
ISBN 978-1-62403-002-4 (pbk.)
1. Earthquakes--Juvenile literature. 2. Natural disasters--Juvenile literature.
I. Title.
551.22--dc23
                                        2013902045

Photo Credits: Youding Xie/iStockphoto, cover, 1; Gerald Herbert/AP Images, 4, 45; Ricardo Arduengo/AP Images, 7; Red Line Editorial, 8; Art Konovalov/Shutterstock Images, 12; Baris Simsek/iStockphoto, 14; Thinkstock, 16, 17; Kyodo News/AP Images, 19; Bill Roth/Anchorage Daily News/AP Images, 20; David Guttenfelder/AP Images, 22; Bedu Saini/AP Images, 25; Arnold Genthe/AP Images, 26; Janet Babb/US Geological Survey, 28; Reed Saxon/AP Images, 30; Ian McKain/AP Images, 32; Shutterstock Images, 34, 37; Larry Steagall/Kitsap Sun/AP Images, 38

CONTENTS

CHAPTER ONE

DISASTER IN HAITI

On January 12, 2010, American Bob Poff was driving his truck on the side of a mountain. The mountain was near Port-au-Prince, the capital city of Haiti. Haiti is a poor country located on the Caribbean island of Hispaniola. Poff worked for the Salvation Army. He and his wife had arrived in Haiti in April 2009. They had fallen in love with the small country and its people.

In January 2010, an earthquake rocked the small island nation of Haiti.

Without warning, Poff's drive took a terrifying turn. The ground began to shake. The violent shaking caused his truck to bounce around the road. Poff thought something had hit his truck. He was scared the truck might tumble off the mountainside.

Poff was actually experiencing Haiti's worst earthquake in more than 200 years. It measured 7.0 in magnitude on the moment magnitude scale. This is a scale scientists use to measure the strength of an earthquake. The shaking lasted less than a minute. But the damage was

How Long Do Earthquakes Last?

Most earthquakes last only a few seconds. A medium to large earthquake may have strong ground shaking for 10 to 30 seconds. In rare cases, an earthquake can shake for a minute or longer. On December 26, 2004, the world's longest-lasting recorded earthquake struck. The Sumatra-Andaman Islands earthquake shook off the coast of Indonesia. The quake lasted more than eight minutes. This earthquake also triggered a deadly tsunami.

Some survivors camped outside the Haitian National Palace, which was destroyed by the quake.

severe. Buildings across the small country had fallen. Houses, shops, schools, hospitals, and government buildings collapsed. Many buildings were damaged or destroyed. These included the National Palace, the National Assembly building, and the Port-au-Prince Cathedral.

Moment Magnitude Scale

Moment Magnitude	How Often (approximate)	Damage
1.0 to 1.9	8,000 per day	None; usually only detected by instruments
2.0 to 2.9	1,000 per day	Little to none
3.0 to 3.9	350 per day	Little to none; may be felt indoors
4.0 to 4.9	13,000 per year	Minor; often felt indoors
5.0 to 5.9	1,300 per year	Considerable; felt by all in the area
6.0 to 6.9	120 per year	Heavy; buildings likely damaged
7.0 to 7.9	17 per year	Severe; widespread damage
8.0 and up	1 per year	Extremely severe; widespread damage and fatalities

Earthquake Magnitude

In 1979 the moment magnitude scale replaced the Richter scale as the system scientists use to measure the size and strength of earthquakes. This chart shows the effects of earthquakes based on the moment magnitude scale and how often they occur. Where does the 2010 Haitian earthquake fall on this chart? How does the chart help you compare the Haitian quake with other earthquakes?

After the quake, people ran into the streets. Many were injured. Some screamed for help. Concrete from the collapsed buildings blocked roads. Emergency workers could not travel on roads to reach people who had been injured. Survivors had no working phones, water, or power.

Aftershocks, small earthquakes that follow major earthquakes, continued shaking the ground. Some aftershocks measured 5.0 or greater in magnitude. The night after the earthquake, many people in Haiti slept in the streets, on pavement, in cars, or in makeshift tents. Many people's homes had been destroyed. Others

Haiti's Buildings

Haiti is a very poor country. Many buildings and houses were cheaply constructed. These buildings were not built to withstand a major earthquake. The 2010 quake caused many Haitian buildings to collapse within seconds. Many of these buildings' walls were made of stacked bricks or concrete blocks. These were easily knocked loose during the earthquake.

were afraid to go back inside buildings that were still standing. They were worried the shaking might bring down even more buildings.

The 2010 earthquake was especially devastating because it struck just 15 miles (24 km) southwest of Port-au-Prince. This is the most populated area of Haiti. Nobody knows exactly how many people were killed in the Haitian earthquake. Officials estimate that between 50,000 and 316,000 people died. The earthquake injured another 300,000 people. More than 220,000 homes were destroyed or badly damaged. As many as 1.3 million people had to find a new place to live. It was the worst natural disaster in Haiti's history.

Bob Poff experienced the Haitian earthquake firsthand. He described what happened in a Salvation Army blog:

> When the earthquake struck, I was driving down the mountain from Pétionville. Our truck was being tossed to and fro like a toy, and when it stopped, I looked out the windows to see buildings "pancaking" down, like I have never witnessed before. Traffic, of course, came to a stand-still, while thousands of people poured out into the streets, crying, carrying bloody bodies, looking for anyone who could help them. We piled as many bodies into the back of our truck, and took them down the hill with us, hoping to find medical attention. All of them were older, scared, bleeding, and terrified. It took about 2 hours to go less than 1 mile. Traffic was horrible, devastation was everywhere, and suffering humanity was front and center.

Source: Bob Poff. "Devastation in Haiti, A First-Hand Account." January 13, 2010. The Salvation Army. The Salvation Army in Canada, 2013. Web. Accessed January 4, 2013.

Back It Up

In this passage, Poff is using evidence to support a point. Write a paragraph describing the point Poff is making. Then write down two or three pieces of evidence he uses to make the point.

CHAPTER TWO

BENEATH THE SURFACE

Like all earthquakes, the 2010 Haitian earthquake began deep inside the earth. The earth has three main layers. The outer layer is the crust. The crust is the ground on which we stand. It includes rocks, soil, and seabed. Beneath the ocean, the crust is about five miles (8 km) thick. Under the continents, the crust is thicker. Continental crust is about 30 miles (50 km) thick.

Earthquakes cause a great deal of damage on the surface, but they begin deep within the earth.

The earth's interior has several layers.

The mantle is the layer that sits underneath the crust. It's about 1,800 miles (2,900 km) thick. In some parts, the mantle rock is so hot that it melts. The melting rock forms a thick liquid called magma.

The mantle layer surrounds the earth's core. The core has two parts. The outer core is made of hot, liquid metal. Scientists believe the outer core's temperature is about 7,200 to 9,000 degrees Fahrenheit (4,000–5,000°C). The inner core is even hotter. Scientists estimate that the inner core is about

9,000 to 13,000 degrees Fahrenheit (5,000–7,000°C). The pressure inside the inner core is so high it cannot melt into a liquid. It is a solid iron-nickel ball.

Moving Pieces

Earth's crust and part of the upper mantle are broken into pieces called tectonic plates. Tectonic plates float on top of the mantle. The plates move very slowly, usually less than one inch (2.5 cm) each year.

When tectonic plates move apart, they form a gap called a rift. Magma slowly flows from the mantle into the rift. This magma cools and hardens to form new land or seabed. Sometimes tectonic plates collide. One plate can slide over another plate. Other times, two plates push

Ring of Fire
The Ring of Fire is an area shaped like a horseshoe that stretches around the Pacific Ocean. The edges of several large tectonic plates meet along the Ring of Fire. Earthquakes are most likely to happen near the edges of the earth's plates. The Ring of Fire is the most active area in the world for earthquakes.

The Himalayan Mountains in Asia were formed when two of Earth's plates crashed together.

against each other with great force. The land may rise upward to form mountains.

Faults

The edges of tectonic plates are called plate boundaries. These are the places where plates move apart, slide over each other, slide past each other, or push against each other. This movement causes pressure to build up in the rocks near the plate boundaries. This pressure causes cracks, called faults, in the earth's crust. Most faults occur at plate boundaries. But sometimes faults can open up in the middle of plates.

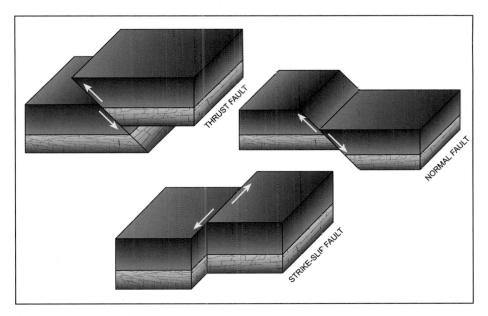

Geologic Faults

Cracks in Earth's crust that form between moving rock are called faults. Not all faults look the same. This diagram shows three basic types of faults and how they move. How might these different types of movement create different kinds of earthquakes?

There are different types of faults. Not all faults are active. Some faults are ancient and may have caused earthquakes millions of years ago. But these faults are quiet today.

When Plates Break Apart

The earth's plates often push, pull, and scrape against each other. But plate edges are rough. Sometimes the edges stick together while the rest of a plate keeps

San Andreas Fault

The San Andreas Fault is a large fault in California. It measures about 800 miles (1,300 km) long. It formed approximately 28 million years ago. That's when the Pacific Plate and the North American Plate began moving in different directions. In 1906 the plates shifted along the fault and caused the great San Francisco earthquake.

moving. When plate edges along a fault get stuck, energy that would normally cause the plates to slide past each other builds up. Eventually the edges break free. The rock cracks and shifts. This causes an earthquake.

Seismic Waves

The rock's sudden movement releases waves of energy, known as seismic waves. The energy moves outward from the fault in all directions. The waves shake the ground as they move through it.

The point beneath the earth's surface where an earthquake begins is its focus. The point on the surface directly above the focus is the quake's epicenter. An earthquake's waves of energy are strongest at its epicenter. The waves lose strength

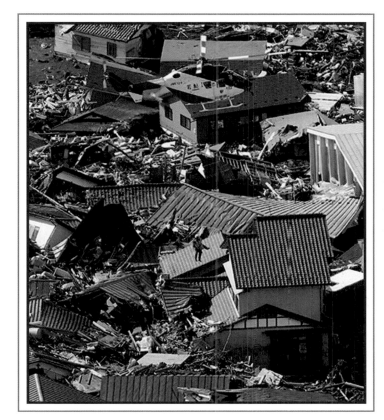

In 2011 a major earthquake hit Japan. This caused a tsunami. Together, the tsunami and earthquake caused as much as $309 billion in damage.

as they move away. Weaker waves cause less ground shaking farther from an earthquake's epicenter.

Several types of seismic waves occur during an earthquake. Some move inside the earth. Others move along the earth's surface. Seismic waves can knock down buildings and trigger tsunamis. These are large ocean waves. A major earthquake with strong seismic waves can cause much destruction, injury, and death.

CHAPTER THREE

EFFECTS OF EARTHQUAKES

When most people think of an earthquake, they picture the ground shaking violently. The shaking can cause objects to fall from shelves or tip over. Street signs or traffic lights fall. Power lines topple. The shaking may open huge cracks in the ground. If the shaking is strong enough, buildings might even collapse. Collapsed buildings cause most deaths in an earthquake.

In 2002 an earthquake in Alaska was strong enough to pull apart the road.

In May 2008, a 7.9 magnitude earthquake struck China's Sichuan province. The shaking caused landslides. Falling rock blocked narrow mountain roads and buried entire villages.

Landslides and Avalanches

Ground shaking during an earthquake can trigger landslides in hilly or mountainous areas. The shaking can loosen rocks that tumble down a slope. The falling rocks block roads and damage buildings. Dirt, mud, and other debris also shake loose. Sometimes a landslide is large enough to bury houses and buildings.

In snowy areas, earthquakes can shake the snow loose and cause avalanches. These large masses of falling snow and ice can bury buildings, roads, and even entire towns.

Soil Liquefaction

Another dangerous effect of earthquakes is soil liquefaction. This usually occurs in areas where soil is moist and loosely packed. When the ground shakes, this already-loose soil becomes unstable and fluid. The soil acts like quicksand. Buildings sink into the ground or tilt sideways. Surfaces shift and slopes slide. Roadways and sidewalks buckle. Soil liquefaction can cause millions of dollars of damage.

Tsunamis

Some earthquakes trigger deadly tsunamis. Earthquakes on the ocean floor cause most tsunamis. During the quake, the ocean floor shifts. The movement

Sinking Ground

In March 2011, a magnitude 9.0 earthquake hit Japan. Soil liquefaction caused entire buildings to tilt and sink. The fluid soil damaged water, sewer, and gas pipelines. In some places, the ground sank as much as four feet (1.2 m).

often causes a water wave. This wave can move as fast as a jet airplane. As the wave moves toward shore, the tsunami grows taller. It can form a huge wall of water up to 100 feet (30 m) high. When the massive wave hits land, it sometimes does major damage to the coastline. The water can flood villages for many miles inland.

Deadly Tsunami

In December 2004, a magnitude 9.1 earthquake struck near the west coast of northern Sumatra, Indonesia. The earthquake, known as the Sumatra-Andaman Islands earthquake, triggered a massive tsunami in the Indian Ocean. The tsunami flooded entire towns and villages. It killed approximately 230,000 people.

Fires

A powerful earthquake can also cause destructive fires. Ground shaking sometimes damages pipes carrying natural gas. If the gas escapes, it can catch on fire. Damaged power lines and tipped-over wood or coal stoves can also start fires. If roads are blocked or damaged, firefighters may

The streets of Banda Aceh, Indonesia, flooded with seawater from a tsunami just moments after the 2004 earthquake hit.

have a hard time reaching the fire. If the earthquake damages water lines, the firefighters may not have enough water to put out the fire. Flames can spread quickly and destroy entire neighborhoods.

In 1906 fires caused by a powerful earthquake destroyed most of San Francisco. On April 18, a magnitude 7.9 earthquake struck early in the morning. Soon after the quake, fire erupted in the city's business district. The fire quickly spread through the

The 1906 fire in San Francisco burned for three days after an earthquake.

city. By the time the fires finally went out, more than 3,000 people had died.

Earthquakes are often dangerous because they are nearly impossible to predict. Still, scientists around the world spend their lives studying these dangerous natural disasters. Scientists hope that by learning more about earthquakes, they will be able to understand how they behave. This information will help save lives.

Poet Lawrence Harris wrote the poem "Re-buildin'" about rebuilding the city of San Francisco after the 1906 San Francisco earthquake and fire:

> . . .
>
> There's shirt sleeves everywhere you go.
>> top boots and overalls.
> And the men are all a scrapin'
>> with their backs agin' the walls.
> A workin' and a strivin'
>> and a buildin' up a town
> That no strength of future furies
>> can ever batter down.
>
> . . .

Source: Harris, Lawrence W. "Re-buildin'." 1906. *The 1906 San Francisco Earthquake and Fire. The Regents of the University of California, 2007.* Web. Accessed January 7, 2013.

What's the Big Idea?

Take a closer look at the excerpt of Harris's poem shown above. What is he trying to say about the people working to rebuild San Francisco? Pick out two details Harris uses to make his point.

CHAPTER FOUR

STUDYING EARTHQUAKES

The ability to predict earthquakes could save many lives. Scientists study patterns of past earthquakes. They study changes in the water table, stream flow, and patterns of electrical currents in the ground. They look at potential warning signals such as foreshocks, small earthquakes that come before a larger earthquake. Some scientists even study animal behavior. Yet so far, no methods

Scientists study the earth's movement at seismic stations around the world, including this one on the volcano Kilauea in Hawaii. A series of earthquakes is often a sign that a volcano is about to erupt.

Scientists study evidence of past earthquakes to better understand future earthquakes.

of predicting earthquakes have worked. Even so, scientists continue studying earthquakes. They hope that one day they will be able to predict the next big one before it happens.

Scientists who study earthquakes are known as seismologists. They pay close attention to faults near places where earthquakes might occur. Seismologists cannot accurately say exactly when an earthquake will occur. But they can give predictions about how often a certain fault is likely to rupture.

Seismologists place instruments called creepmeters and global positioning systems (GPS) near faults. They use these tools to look for movements in the earth's crust. Seismologists also use instruments called seismographs. A seismograph creates a recording called a seismogram.

Scientists have placed seismograph stations all over the world. These stations monitor the earth's

Animals and Earthquakes

In ancient Greece, people noticed that rats, weasels, snakes, and centipedes left their homes and moved to safety several days before a large earthquake. In modern times, people have also reported that animals behave strangely before an earthquake. Some people believe this behavior proves animals can sense an earthquake before it strikes. Other scientists believe there is no connection between animal behavior and earthquakes. What do you think?

Seismographs measure the ground vibrations during an earthquake.

crust for movement that may signal an earthquake. Seismologists also use seismographs to pinpoint exactly where an earthquake starts. By comparing seismograms from different places, scientists can determine an earthquake's epicenter.

Measuring Earthquakes

Scientists use two scales to measure how strong an earthquake is. The moment magnitude scale measures the magnitude of a quake. Higher numbers equal bigger quakes.

The modified Mercalli intensity scale measures an earthquake's intensity. The intensity is the effect the earthquake has on the earth's surface. The intensity of shaking depends on where you are during an earthquake. Mercalli ratings are based on people's descriptions of an earthquake's damage and effects. The Mercalli scale uses a 12-point rating scale. A higher number equals greater intensity. An earthquake's intensity depends on how close you are to the epicenter. This means a single earthquake may have different intensity ratings.

FURTHER EVIDENCE

Chapter Four covers how scientists study earthquakes. What is one of the chapter's main points? What are some pieces of evidence in the chapter that support this main point? Check out the US Geological Survey Web site at the link below. Find a quote from the Web site that supports this chapter's main point. Write a few sentences using the new information from the Web site as evidence to support this main point.

The Science of Earthquakes
www.mycorelibrary.com/earthquakes

CHAPTER FIVE

GETTING READY

When the ground shakes during an earthquake, a building's foundation can move. Walls made from brick or concrete blocks can shake apart. Roofs fall down. Sometimes entire buildings collapse. Scientists cannot predict earthquakes. But they study ways to keep people safer during an earthquake.

One of the greatest earthquake dangers comes from falling buildings.

Quakeproof Building

In October 1989, a magnitude 7.1 earthquake struck Northern California. In San Francisco, the 49-story Transamerica Pyramid office building shook for more than a minute. The top floor swayed more than one foot (0.3 m) from side to side. But the building's earthquake-proof design worked as planned. The building was not damaged, and no one was seriously injured.

Safer Buildings

To make buildings safer, engineers study how structures react to earthquakes. They place special instruments in structures and on the ground nearby. Then they measure how the structure reacts during an earthquake. Every time there is an earthquake, engineers get new information. Using this information, engineers have improved designs for buildings, bridges, and other structures.

Strong materials, such as steel, reinforce buildings. This helps them stay intact during an earthquake. Buildings with a larger base and a smaller top are more likely to stay standing. Short buildings

The Transamerica Pyramid office building, right, in San Francisco is designed to withstand powerful earthquakes.

Students at an elementary school in Washington State practice taking cover during an earthquake safety drill.

are also more likely to survive an earthquake. This is because shaking is more intense on higher floors. A flexible support between a building and its foundation can also help during an earthquake. If the foundation shakes sideways, the support moves the opposite way. The building might sway, but it will not collapse.

Earthquake Safety

If you are in an earthquake, there are a few things you can do to stay safe. If you are inside, you should immediately drop to the ground. Take cover under a sturdy piece of furniture, and hold on until the shaking

Earthquake Emergency Kit

Many people live in areas where earthquakes are common. But earthquakes can happen almost anywhere. You should be ready if an earthquake strikes your home. Experts recommend these items for a basic earthquake emergency kit:

- Bottled water
- Nonperishable food
- Flashlight and batteries
- A battery-powered radio
- First aid kit
- Whistle
- Blankets
- Can opener

ends. If there is no table or desk nearby, take cover in an inside corner of the building. Stay away from glass, windows, outside walls, and doors. You don't want to be near anything that could fall over.

If you are outside when the earthquake begins, find an area away from buildings, streetlights, and power lines. Be on the lookout for falling rock or snow that could be triggered by the earthquake.

After the ground stops shaking, look around to make sure it is safe to move. Make your way to a safe area. Be aware of fire. Avoid any downed power lines. Be ready for aftershocks. Aftershocks can be strong enough to cause more

The Biggest Quake

The largest recorded earthquake occurred in Chile in 1960. It measured 9.5 in magnitude. The earthquake itself killed more than 1,500 people and left approximately 2 million people homeless. The quake also triggered a large tsunami that caused damage and death as far away as Hawaii and Japan.

damage, especially when structures are already weakened from the first earthquake. Aftershocks can happen in the hours, days, weeks, and months after the earthquake.

Earthquakes have been shaking our planet for millions of years. They strike without warning. But seismologists learn more from each new earthquake. Understanding earthquakes' causes and effects will help us be ready when the earth lets loose its next big quake.

EXPLORE ONLINE

The Web site below has even more information about preparing for an earthquake. As you know, every source is different. Reread Chapter Five of this book. What are the similarities between Chapter Five and the information you found on the Web site? How do the two sources present information differently?

Staying Safe in an Earthquake
www.mycorelibrary.com/earthquakes

TEN DEVASTATING EARTHQUAKES

January 1700
North Pacific Coast of America: Magnitude 9.0 (estimated)
Native Americans near Vancouver Island described how the large Native American community of Pachena Bay was wiped out by a huge wave triggered by the earthquake. The quake also triggered a tsunami that was recorded as far away as Japan, more than 4,000 miles (6,400 km) away.

November 1755
Lisbon, Portugal: Magnitude 8.7
An earthquake, tsunami, and fire caused the almost total destruction of the city of Lisbon. One fourth of the city's people were killed.

August 1868
Arica, Peru (now part of Chile): Magnitude 9.0 (estimated)
This quake triggered a tsunami that destroyed the city of Arequipa, Peru, and killed approximately 25,000 people.

April 1906
Northern California: Magnitude 7.9
This rupturing of the San Andreas Fault in 1906 triggered a famous earthquake, best known for the damage it caused in San Francisco, California. The quake also triggered a fire that burned much of the city of San Francisco to the ground. More than 3,000 lives were lost in the disaster.

May 1960
Chile: Magnitude 9.5
The world's most powerful earthquake left more than 4,000 people dead or injured and 2 million homeless after it struck southern Chile.

March 1964

*Prince William Sound,
Alaska: Magnitude 9.2*
This quake caused landslides in
Anchorage and devastated The
Gulf of Alaska. It triggered a
tsunami and caused 128 deaths
and $311 million of damage.

December 2004

*Off Northern Sumatra:
Magnitude 9.1*
This massive earthquake triggered
the deadliest tsunami in history.
It affected 14 countries across
Asia and east Africa and killed
approximately 230,000 people.

January 2010

Haiti: Magnitude 7.0
This was Haiti's worst earthquake
in more than 200 years. It killed
more than 50,000 people and left
hundreds of thousands of people
homeless.

February 2010

*Off the Coast of Bio-Bio,
Chile: Magnitude 8.8*
This quake generated a Pacific-
wide tsunami. It killed more than
500 people and injured thousands.

March 2011

*Off East Coast of Honchu,
Japan: Magnitude 9.0*
This quake and resulting tsunami
killed more than 15,000 people
and significantly damaged
buildings, roads, bridges, and
railways along the east coast of
Japan.

Surprise Me

Chapter Three of this book discusses what causes earthquakes. The way earthquakes form can be interesting and surprising. After reading this book, what two or three facts about earthquakes did you find most surprising? Write a few sentences about each fact. Why did you find them surprising?

Why Do I Care?

Earthquakes are more common in certain areas of the world. Even if you don't live in a high-risk earthquake area, you can still find similarities between your life and those living in earthquake zones. How can earthquakes affect your life today? Are there things that you will not be able to do or products you will not be able to buy if an earthquake strikes a certain area? How might your life be different if a massive earthquake hit the United States? Use your imagination!

You Are There

This book discusses the devastating effects of earthquakes. Imagine that you are a boy or girl living near the Ring of Fire. The ground begins to shake. What do you do? What will you do after the shaking ends?

Take a Stand

Do you think people should rebuild in earthquake-prone areas? Or should they move to a safer area? Write a short essay explaining your opinion. Make sure to give reasons for your opinion and facts and details that support those reasons.

GLOSSARY

aftershock
a smaller earthquake that
follows a large one

epicenter
the point on the earth's
surface directly above the
place where an earthquake
occurs

fault
a crack in the earth's crust
where the blocks of crust on
either side of the fracture
have moved toward, away
from, or past each other

focus
the point where an
earthquake begins

liquefaction
the process in which
soil becomes fluid-like
and unstable during an
earthquake

magma
hot, liquid rock

magnitude
a measure of the size of an
earthquake

rift
a crack that forms in the
earth's crust as plates move
apart

seismic wave
a wave of energy created by
an earthquake

seismologist
a scientist who studies
earthquakes

tectonic plate
a section of the earth's crust
and part of the upper mantle
that supports continents and
oceans

LEARN MORE

Books

Griffey, Harriet. *Earthquakes and Other Natural Disasters*. DK Readers. New York: Dorling Kindersley, 2010.

McDougall, Chrös. *The San Francisco Earthquake and Fire*. Minneapolis: ABDO, 2013.

Stewart, Melissa. *Earthquakes and Volcanoes*. Washington, DC: Smithsonian, 2008.

Web Links

To learn more about earthquakes, visit ABDO Publishing Company online at **www.abdopublishing.com**. Web sites about earthquakes are featured on our Book Links page. These links are routinely monitored and updated to provide the most current information available. Visit **www.mycorelibrary.com** for free additional tools for teachers and students.

INDEX

ABOUT THE AUTHOR

Carla Mooney is the author of several books for young readers. She loves learning about science. A graduate of the University of Pennsylvania, she lives in Pittsburgh, Pennsylvania, with her husband and three children.